YOUR KNOWLEDGE HAS VALUE

Bibliographic information published by the German National Library:

The German National Library lists this publication in the National Bibliography; detailed bibliographic data are available on the Internet at http://dnb.dnb.de .

Imprint:

Copyright © 2019 GRIN Verlag
Print and binding: Books on Demand GmbH, Norderstedt Germany
ISBN: 9783346209009

This book at GRIN:

https://www.grin.com/document/595187

Anonym

What Benefits Can Artificial Intelligence Bring to the Road Transportation Sector? An Overview

GRIN Verlag

GRIN - Your knowledge has value

Since its foundation in 1998, GRIN has specialized in publishing academic texts by students, college teachers and other academics as e-book and printed book. The website www.grin.com is an ideal platform for presenting term papers, final papers, scientific essays, dissertations and specialist books.

Visit us on the internet:

http://www.grin.com/

http://www.facebook.com/grincom

http://www.twitter.com/grin_com

Table of contents

1 Index of abbreviations

AI   artificial intelligence

ASI   artificial superintelligence

ML   machine learning

2 Introduction

AI is taking on more and more tasks in the everyday world. Talking devices and digital assistants, such as Amazon's Alexa or Apple's Siri give consumers easy access to various forms of AI in order to simplify their everyday lives. The distinction between digital chatbots and people is also getting increasingly more difficult.

On the one hand, as the technology progresses, the feasible utilization of AI to identify patterns, learn from experience and find novel solutions to new challenges, proceeds to prosper. On the other hand, the huge hype that the market is experiencing and the resulting media coverage is being taken advantage of. Plenty of companies are making
use of this opportunity and are rebranding their existing solution to AI (Schrank, Eisele, Lomax & Bak, 2015, p. 7). This leads to the confusion of the public and press.

There are many challenges and inefficiencies we have to face in our lives. These issues could be solved by AI, which is one of the reasons for the great optimism regarding AI. Tasks, which could not be automated in the past, will be automated in the future and thus, will have an enormous effect on society and the economy. One estimation of the AI market claimed a growth from $8 billion in 2016 to $47 Billion in 2020 (Lu, Li, Chen, Kim & Serikawa, 2017, p. 3). Productivity and wealth will beyond doubt elevate. Different types of jobs are going to be affected in miscellaneous ways. Although society should remain focused on the achievable benefits of AI implementation, risks, challenges, and unintended consequences also have to be appropriately taken into consideration.

In this paper, the focus will be on the positive reinforcement of society, for the simple reason that writing about the drawbacks as well, will extend the length of this paper beyond the given guidelines. By way of example, which regulations are needed to ensure the protection of the public and fairness in economic competition and how will employment rates be influenced? Likewise, the history of the development of AI will be left out for the same reason.

On the grounds of the previously mentioned content, I would like to write my paper in the module "Introduction to Intelligence and Security Studies" about AI. Initially, I will present definitions of intelligence and a description of AI and its abilities. The subsequent description of functions and various forms of AI are intended to give an overview of the potential of AI. A

Practical example of the implementation of AI in the Road transport sector, as well as a conclusion, are bringing my paper to a close.

3 Definition of intelligence

The term Intelligence has a long history of research and debate. Yet, a standard definition is still not available.

3.1 Intelligence

"Viewed narrowly, there seem to be almost as many definitions of intelligence as there were experts asked to define it. Viewed broadly, however, two themes seem to run through at least several of these definitions: the capacity to learn from experience, and adaptation to one's environment. Indeed, an earlier definition often cited by these experts viewed intelligence as general adaptability to new problems and conditions of life" (Gregory, 1987, p. 376).

The trend of having as many definitions as there were experts asked to define it continues in 2006. Two researchers collected 70 definitions from organizations, psychologists and researchers in AI. Along with the myriad of definitions, some appearances are more frequent. Because of the commonly occurring features, the extracted definition by Legg and Hutter (2006, p. 8) is the following: "Intelligence measures an agent's ability to achieve goals in a wide range of environments".

The next point I want to mention is the theory of multiple intelligences. The author of this theory claims that there are at least eight autonomous intelligences in every single individual (Moran & Gardner, 2006, p. 213ff). Creating products and solving problems is done by the individual in accordance with the relevance to the society, the individual lives in. It is done individually or collectively by making use of one or more of the several intelligences. Gardner classified the eight intelligences in linguistic, logical- mathematical, spatial, musical, bodily-kinesthetic, naturalistic, interpersonal and intrapersonal intelligence (ebd.). On a rather ironical note, there where even scientists who "have suggested we define intelligence as what intelligence tests measure and get
on with testing it" (Sternberg, 2003, p. 151).

3.2 Kinds of intelligence

Humans differ in the ability to understand and interact with others in a social setting. The capability of comprehension and expression of emotions is also differentiating among people. Therefore, another factor has to be taken into account. The difference between the two kinds of intelligence: social and emotional intelligence.

3.2.1 Emotional intelligence

The ability of correct assessment and influence of feelings in oneself and others is referred to as emotional intelligence. This kind of intelligence is divided into four categories such as perception of emotions (facial expressions, gestures, voices, postures), use of emotions to support thinking (knowledge of the interaction of feelings and thoughts), understanding from emotions (understanding and analyzing emotions) and dealing with emotions (evoking feelings, avoiding and correcting emotional evaluations) (Stangl, 2019).

3.2.2 Social intelligence

Social intelligence is the set of individual attitudes and abilities that are useful in the sense of cooperation to link one's objective with the attitudes and values of another or a group. Social intelligence includes a variety of skills that are useful or necessary for social interaction. Often this term is equated with social competence, whereby social intelligence in this sense is not only reserved for humans but for animals living together in groups, too (Stangl, 2019).

4 Artificial intelligence

A universally accepted definition of AI is also not available. Various fields of science, for instance, computer science, psychology, philosophy, and linguistics are pooled together in the topic of AI. The reason for implementing artificial intelligence is establishing a computer, which can do tasks, which would usually require human intelligence. Since creating a computer with human intelligence is one of the objectives of AI, the definition of intelligence is the groundwork for the definition of AI. The ambiguity and vagueness of the definition of intelligence are therefore reoccurring in the definition of AI.

Having said that, there are many points of view on AI and many definitions are in existence. One approach to the subject of defining AI can be made by dividing into different forms of AI. Assisted intelligence is at the lower end of the spectrum of AI and is used to automate simple tasks to perform these faster and cheaper. Assisted Intelligence falls under the class of "narrow" AI (MIT Technology Review Insights 2019). Augmented intelligence supports people in making better situational decisions. This form of AI is capable of learning and adjusting constantly by receiving data input from the users. In return, humans will be able to make more sound and accurate decisions, based on the information received from the AI (ebd.). Autonomous intelligence is the most advanced form of AI, in which the mere purpose of a human being is the surveillance of the machine, which acts independently, for example, self-driving vehicles (ebd.).

4.1 Functions of artificial intelligence

AI systems can be used for a wide variety of applications and functions. In most cases, AI is used to execute at least one of the following seven general functions.

Monitoring: AI systems can analyze large amounts of data in a very short time and detect deviations and patterns. Since AI systems can do this much faster   often in real time - and more accurately than humans, they are very well suited for surveillance functions, such as cybersecurity and environmental changes (Castro & New 2016, p. 4ff).

> "Discovering: AI can extract valuable insights from large datasets, often referred to as data mining, and discover new solutions through simulations. In particular, because AI uses dynamic models that learn and adapt from data, it is very effective at un-covering abstract patterns and revealing novel insights that traditional computer programs cannot. Predicting: AI can forecast or model how trends are likely to develop in the future, thereby enabling systems to predict, recommend, and personalize responses. Many consumers are likely familiar with these types of applications, such as Netflix's recommendation algorithm, which analyzes users' viewing histories, stated preferences, and other factors to suggest new titles that they might like. Data-intensive applications, such as precision medicine and weather forecasting, stand to benefit from this use of AI.

Interpreting: Until recently, most data analytics has focused on structured data—information that is well organized according to a specific framework, such as a spreadsheet of survey responses. Because AI can learn and identify patterns, it can interpret unstructured data—information that is not easily classifiable, such as images, video, audio, and text. As a result, computer systems are now capable of analyzing dramatically more kinds of information about the world. For example, AI helps smartphone apps interpret voice instructions to schedule meetings, diagnostic software to analyze X-rays to identify aneurysms, and legal software to rapidly analyze court decisions relevant to a particular case.

Interacting with the Physical Environment: AI can facilitate a diverse range of machine-to-environment interactions that allow autonomous systems to directly engage with the physical environment. In particular, AI enables robotic systems that can navigate and manipulate the world around them. For example, autonomous vehicles analyze huge amounts of real-time data from an array of sensors, cameras, GPS systems, and maps to determine a safe and efficient route down a street.

Interacting with People: AI can allow humans to interact more easily with computer systems. Humans typically interact with machines by adjusting their behavior to meet the needs of the computer, such as by typing on a keyboard, pressing a button, or adjusting a dial. With AI, humans can interact with computers the way they do with other people, as computer systems can respond to speech, gestures, and even facial expressions. For example, individuals can ask questions of AI-powered chatbots by having a conversation or beckon a robot to come over with a nod or wave.

Interacting with Machines: AI can automatically coordinate complicated machine-to-machine interactions. For example, a control system for a data center can use AI to continuously monitor computing activity, internal temperature, and environmental conditions, and make adjustments to cooling systems to optimize performance while minimizing energy costs. This ability also allows for multiple separate AI systems to coordinate with each other, such as a fleet of autonomous trucks managing themselves in a platoon formation to reduce fuel consumption, or autonomous robots in a warehouse that communicate with each other to sort and retrieve items" (ebd.).

4.2 Machine Learning

ML and AI are often used as synonyms, which is used to deceive "customers by pro-claiming using AI on their technologies while not being clear about their products' limits" (Iriondo, 2019). In 2019 there was a report that claimed, "forty percent of 'AI startups' in Europe don't use AI" (Vincent, 2019). When we look back at my description of AI, the confusion which subsists in the media and the public is not a complete surprise. The computer scientist and ML pioneer Mitchell (1997) defined ML as "the study of computer algorithms that allow computer programs to automatically improve through experience" hence it is a branch of AI.

ML is utilized by giving the AI system an available data set, which is divided into three groups: training data, validation data, and test data. The AI system uses the training data to build a model with the relevant functions. Subsequently, the validation data is used to screen the model for propriety. Thereupon, the achieved precision or performance of the outcome requires verification, which is accomplished through the test data. This continually evolving model is a mathematical structure that identifies a range of possible decision-making principles with adaptable parameters.

One necessity of ML is the implementation of an objective function. This will aid in evaluating the desirability of the outcome, which results from the selection of parameters by the machine. The objective function integrates parts of a reward mechanism, by which the machine receives a reward for achieving good findings, as well as for the application of simpler rules. Rewarding the machine for desirable outcomes is causing the machine to select the parameters, which are maximizing the objective function. The repetition and readjustment of the parameters, based on the data given to the machine, eventuates in approaching the maximization of the objective function and thus, the acquired training values are growing increasingly better and more accurate.

A trained model that can generalize and still deliver precise results on future cases that it has never seen before, is the goal of ML. In other words, ML is not meant to solve a specific problem, but rather an attempt to find solutions for various issues.

4.3 Deep learning

How can a human write an essay in the English language, although his native language is German while switching between English and German literature and still being able to understand the context unconsciously? The connection between the biological neural network and the nervous system in the human body is the answer. Every Neuron in the human brain is connected to ten thousand other neurons. This yields a complex network with over 85 billion neurons (Cherry, 2019). A message from one neuron to another neuron is passed on via receiving and transferring an electrochemical signal. On account of this structure and functionality, the concept of deep learning was inspired.

Deep learning is a newer subfield of ML. It is based on a network of nodes, which are interconnected via differently weighted lines. These nodes are symbolizing the neurons in the human brain and are arranged in multiple layers – sometimes more than 100 – with a large number of nodes per layer. Recognizing extremely complex and precise patterns in data is made possible by structuring the nodes in such an array.

4.4 Narrow AI vs general AI

AI has reached the vast majority of people who have a smartphone in their possession since almost every smartphone has some kind of AI implemented. How many people might that be? Based on information from the global smartphone penetration data, there are now over 8.98 Billion mobile connections worldwide, which surpasses the current world population of 7.69 Billion" ("How many phones are in the world", 2019). This leads to a percentage of 66.72 of unique mobile users, which are approximately 5.1 Billion individuals (ebd.). The film industry has put the thought of fear of global dominance by AI or annihilation of the human kind into the minds of society and is therefore ubiquitous, hence a distinction among AI in terms of the degree of autonomy is essential.

"Narrow AI" is used only for specific and defined tasks, "general AI" is a hypothetical form of AI, which can reach or exceed human intelligence. This would imply an application of the problem-solving ability to any kind of problem, such as the ability to learn to drive a car or writing program code, just as a human can (Van Duin & Bakhshl, 2018, p. 6). The reason why there are many fears relating to AI is the very fact of an AI reaching or exceeding human intelligence.

I will now outline the narrow and general AI in more detail. The most limiting form of AI and simultaneously the current state of the art is the narrow AI. Depending on the case of utilization, the narrow AI can perform specific tasks excellently by combining complex algorithms, ML, deep learning and many other techniques (Dickson, 2017). For instance, natural language recognition techniques are often involved, when interactions with humans are taking place like an interplay with the virtual assistant Siri that is part of Apple. The narrow AI relies on ML algorithms, which require huge datasets and an adaptation to the specific usage of this very AI.

The development of general AI is still in its infancy, but when it is developed, it is assumed to reach the intelligence level of people and it will thus be able to carry out assignments that normally only a human could conduct. This AI will then receive the name "Human-Level AI" ("Human-Level AI", 2014). In order to achieve this form of AI, a hardware is mandatory. This Hardware needs to be equivalent to the capacity of the human brain, which means the following: being able to calculate 10 quadrillion calculations per second with an energy output of merely 20 watts. Since 2013 a computer with such high computing power has been in existence. Tianhe-2 is located in China and can perform 34 quadrillion calculations per second (von der Weiden, 2014). However, with an area of approximately 760 square meters, which equals the space of three tennis courts, an energy consumption of 24 megawatts, which is analogous to the energy output of a town and costs of $390, it is not worthwhile for general utilization (ebd.). Despite the physical magnitude of this computer, the software exposes itself to be the bigger issue.

The challenge to create software as advanced as the human brain remains unsolved to this day. Therefore, the most promising method seems to be a programmed AI that can self-modify by self-written code to continually improve (Greene, 2019). Basically, such an AI would mimic the way human biology rewires the brain for the purpose of learning new things. This would allow the AI to become increasingly intelligent and constantly improve its intelligence, which would give rise to exponential enhancement of its intelligence. By 2020, China expects full operational capability of Tianhe-3, which is said to have a 28-times greater computing power than Tianhe-2 ("China baut mal wieder schnellsten Computer der Welt", 2017). One can only guess what will be possible with this new supercomputer.

The ASI stands above the general AI and illustrates a form of AI that is more intelligent than humans. After the general AI is developed completely, the ASI could occur shortly afterward, due to the possibility of exponential evolution of intelligence. This suggests, that in a short period of time, this AI could be billions of times more intelligent than humans. We, as humans, could, by definition, not predict the consequences, as the ASI would outstrip man's intelligence (Loeffler, 2019). With progressing technology improvements like faster computer systems (Tianhe-3) and the emergence of new theories, on how to design and educate deep learning networks, the success of AI and ML will continue to exceed expectations (Genc, 2019). Merely the imagination of such rapid self-development of machines that can program and improve themselves gives rise to questions and concerns concerning how this kind of sophisticated AI would interact with humanity.

5 Road transport sector

Commuting can be a tedious endeavor. By using the service of public transportation, multiple modes of transportation are often required to do a single trip, for instance getting to a train station, go by train to the ideal stop and finally walking or using a ride-share service to the intended destination. If you are commuting by car, you always have to reckon with difficulties along the way to your workplace to be on time. By way of example, construction work, accidents and weather conditions. These instances can constrain traffic flow in a blink of an eye. To enhance the experience of commuting, I will now outline two feasible applications of AI in the road transport sector, which are namely "autonomous public transportation" and "smart traffic signals". These two examples are not realized in the real world yet. They were simulated by computer algorithms.

5.1 Autonomous public transportation

In order to show the massive magnitude of available room for improvement in terms of efficiency, effectiveness, and productivity, as well as psychological and environmental aspects in the transportation section, an example follows:

In 2015, a report by the Texas Transportation Institute stated that there was an estimated $160 billion loss of productivity, due to "42 hours of rush-hour traffic delay per commuter in 2014" (Schrank, Eisele, Lomax & Bak, 2015, p. 7). With a full work week per year wasted through traffic delays, it is crystal clear that AI and ML can bring about a practical, visible and significant shift to the life of humankind.

AI and ML combined with autonomous public transportation and smart traffic lights can not only "reduce the number of taxis on the road by up to 75%" but also reduce waiting time by 40%, as well as reduce overall travel time by 26% (Conner-Simons, 2016).

This may sound like an unreliable marketing phrase, but a study published in 2016, "suggests that using carpooling options from companies like Uber and Lyft could reduce the number of taxis on the road [by] 75 percent without significantly impacting travel time" (ebd.). The researcher of this study generated an algorithm, which discovered that "3,000 four-passenger cars could serve 98 percent of taxi demand in New York City, with an average wait-time of only 2.7 minutes" (ebd.). Additionally, another model of the same research team estimated that compared to the nearly 14,000 taxis in New York City, around 2,000 ten-person cars would be sufficient enough to satisfy 95 % of the taxi demand (ebd.).

This is made possible by transporting two to ten people at once instead of only one. Not only will this take less time and fewer trips to achieve the same monetary value, but also psychological and environmental factors are going to be enhanced. Take, for example, the reduced working shifts for drivers, whereas simultaneously less traffic, less stressful commutes and cleaner air are created.

Another factor worth mentioning is the rerouting of cars. The transportation service can be accelerated by 20% by dispatching idle cars to areas with high demand, based on data from 3 million taxi rides (ebd.).

5.2 Smart traffic signals

Having depicted the autonomous public transportation, I shall now outline another aspect, which can enhance transportation even further – smart traffic signals.

A simulated pilot project in Pittsburgh was aiming to diminish harmful vehicle emissions and long travel times. They succeeded with reductions of 40 percent in the vehicle waiting time, "journey times by as much as 25%, and emissions by up to 20%" ("Pittsburgh cuts travel time by 25% with smart traffic lights", 2017). This great success is entitled to drafts from the field of AI and traffic history, which rendered communication between traffic lights possible. A real-time collaborative adaption of traffic signals to actual traffic conditions was the first attained step. A subsequent demonstration of the traffic lights' "ability to react to quickly changing conditions, reducing traffic congestion and the resulting extra vehicle emissions" was successful, too (ebd.).

Having outlined all these benefits of autonomous public transportation and smart traffic lights, it is clearly obvious that these innovations are earning a high weight in terms of heightened efficiency, productivity as well as in environmental and psychological aspects.

6 Conclusion

All in all, one can say that the annotated road transport sector in this paper is only scratching the surface of the broad spectrum of possible future transformations linked
to the ascending penetrating power of AI. With the adoption of AI, transformations are going to happen in every aspect of life. The innovations in the public and private sectors, driven by AI, are generating outstanding social and economic value. Given ramifications on the transportation section, will, on the one hand, be illustrated by diminished traffic congestion, pollution, and energy consumption. On the other hand, they will augment the well-being of drivers and passengers, by dint of lessened working shifts for drivers. Concurrently, less traffic and less stressful commutes and honed safety and air quality are created.

We have to keep in mind that regular car traffic and aviation were not even considered while conducting the mentioned simulations. Additionally, AI and ML are improving over time, the more they are getting applied, which makes them extremely reliable to change.

Without a doubt, the emergence of fear of change and fear of impact in society will be inevitable, due to the ambiguity and unpredictability of the exceptional ability of AI. Nevertheless, the advancement of AI, referring to the development of AI and adaption to AI, should remain zeroed in on.

There is only one point left to voice. With AI becoming more and more assimilated into our lives, it can even perhaps give rise to a second industrial revolution.

7 List of literature

(2019). *How many phones are in the world*. Retrieved from https://www.bankmycell.com/blog/how-many-phones-are-in-the-world

(2019, June 12). *Human-Level AI*. Retrieved from https://aiimpacts.org/human-level-ai/

(2019, June 15). *Pittsburgh cuts travel time by 25% with smart traffic lights*. Retrieved from https://apolitical.co/solution_article/pittsburgh-cuts-travel-time-25-smart-traffic-lights/

(2019, June 16). *China baut mal wieder schnellsten Computer der Welt*. Retrieved from https://www.spiegel.de/netzwelt/gadgets/tianhe-3-china-baut-neuen-su percomputer-mal-wieder-a-1135380.html

Castro, D., & New, J. (2016). *The Promise of Artificial Intelligence*. Center for data innovation.

Cherry, K. (2019, June 16). *How Many Neurons Are in the Brain?*. Retrieved from https://www.verywellmind.com/how-many-neurons-are-in-the-brain-2794889

Conner-Simons, A. (2019, June 16). *Study: carpooling apps could reduce taxi traffic 75%*. Retrieved from https://www.csail.mit.edu/news/study-carpooling-apps-could-reduce-taxi-traffic-75

Dickson, B. (2019, June 15). *What is Narrow, General and Super Artificial Intelli gence*. Retrieved from https://bdtechtalks.com/2017/05/12/what-is-narrow-general-and-super-artificial-intelligence/

Genc, Ö. (2019, June 11). *Notes on Artificial Intelligence, Machine Learning and Deep Learning for curious people*. Retrieved from https://towardsdatasci ence.com/notes-on-artificial-intelligence-ai-machine-learning-ml-and-deep-learning-dl-for-56e51a2071c2

Greene, T. (2019, June 15). *Google's AI can create better machine-learning code than the researchers who made it*. Retrieved from https://thenextweb.com/ar tificial-intelligence/2017/10/16/googles-ai-can-create-better-machine-learn ing-code-than-the-researchers-who-made-it/

Gregory, R. (1987). *The Oxford Companion to the Mind*. New York: Oxford Univer sity Press.

Iriondo, R. (2019, June 8). *Differences Between AI and Machine Learning, and Why it Matters*. Retrieved from https://medium.com/datadriveninvestor/differ ences-between-ai-and-machine-learning-and-why-it-matters-1255b182fc6

Legg, S., & Hutter, M. (2006). *A Collection of Definitions of Intelligence*. Switzer land.

Loeffler, J. (2019, June 12). *Should We Fear Artificial Superintelligence?*. Retrieved from https://interestingengineering.com/should-we-fear-artificial-superintelli gence

Lu, H., & Li, Y., & Chen, M., & Kim, H., & Serikawa, S. (2017). *Brain Intelligence: Go beyond Artificial Intelligence*. Luxemburg: Springer Science+Business Media.

MIT Technology Review Insights (2019, June 4). *AI Drives Better Business Deci sions*. Retrieved from https://www.technologyreview.com/s/601732/ai-drives-better-business-decisions/

Mitchell, T. (2019, June 13). *Machine Learning*. Retrieved from http://www.cs.cmu.edu/afs/cs.cmu.edu/user/mitchell/ftp/mlbook.html

Moran, S., & Gardner, H. (2006). *Multiple intelligences in the workplace*. In Gard ner, *Multiple intelligences: New horizons* (pp. 213-232). New York: Basic Books.

Schrank, D., & Eisele, B., & Lomax, T., & Bak, J. (2015). *2015 Urban Mobility Scorecard*. Texas: Texas A&M Transportation Institute.

Stangl, W. (2019, June 2). *emotionale Intelligenz*. Retrieved from https://lex ikon.stangl.eu/3239/emotionale-intelligenz/

Stangl, W. (2019, June 2). *soziale Intelligenz*. Retrieved from https://lex ikon.stangl.eu/16329/soziale-intelligenz/

Sternberg, R. (2003). *Intelligence*. In Freedheim, D., & Weiner, I. (2003): *Handbook of Psychology: Volume 1, History of Psychology*. New Jersey.

Van Duin, S., & Bakhshi, N. (2018). *Artificial Intelligence*. Netherlands: Deloitte.

Vincent, J. (2019, June 10). *Forty percent of 'AI startups' in Europe don't actually use AI, claims report*. Retrieved from https://www.theverge.com/2019/3/5/ 18251326/ai-startups-europe-fake-40-percent-mmc-report

von der Weiden, S. (2019, June 16). *„Tianhe-2" braucht so viel Strom wie eine Kleinstadt"*. Retrieved from https://www.welt.de/wissenschaft/arti cle129619300/Tianhe-2-braucht-so-viel-Strom-wie-eine-Kleinstadt.html